D0666530

Managing Teams

Pocket Mentor Series

The Pocket Mentor Series offers immediate solutions to common challenges managers face on the job every day. Each book in the series is packed with handy tools, self-tests, and real-life examples to help you identify your strengths and weaknesses and hone critical skills. Whether you're at your desk, in a meeting, or on the road, these portable guides enable you to tackle the daily demands of your work with greater speed, savvy, and effectiveness.

Books in the series:

Managing
Teams
Expert Solutions to
Everyday Challenges

Harvard Business Review Press

Boston, Massachusetts

Portions of this work were originally published in the book *Team Talk: The Power of Language in Team Dynamics* by Anne Donnellon (Harvard Business School Press, 1996).

Library of Congress Cataloging-in-Publication Data

Managing teams : expert solutions to everyday challenges.
     p. cm. — (Pocket mentor series)
   Includes bibliographical references.
   ISBN 978-1-4221-2974-6 (pbk. : alk. paper)   1. Teams in the workplace—Management.   I. Harvard Business School. Press.
   HD66.M354 2010
   658.4'022—dc22

                                                    2010006807
The paper used in this publication meets the requirements of the American National Standard for Permanence of Paper for Publications and Documents in Libraries and Archives Z39.48-1992.

Contents

Obstacle 3: Poor Communication   23

Ideas for examining one of your processes.

Obstacle 4: Ineffective Team Leadership   29

Strategies for tackling this troubling condition.

Obstacle 5: Destructive Conflict   37

Suggestions for turning unproductive disagreements into productive ones.

Tips and Tools

Mentor's Message: Why Effective Team Management Matters

One of your most crucial responsibilities as a manager is to inspire the best possible performance from your team. After all, being a manager is all about getting things done through others. But managing a team isn't the same as managing individuals. It requires deliberate planning, mindful observation and analysis, and skillful coordination to get individuals to collaborate effectively and efficiently. There's a host of obstacles that can cause even a highly skilled team to stumble. These obstacles range from lack of team identity, low participation, poor communication, and absence of creativity to "groupthink," destructive conflict, and ineffective decision making. And though it may be hard to admit, ineffective leadership from you can present yet another obstacle to your team's progress.

The good news is that there are many techniques and practices you can apply to remove each and every one of these obstacles—and thus position your team for success. In this book, we'll delve into the details of each obstacle—what causes it, and why it's bad news for your team. And we'll present strategies for surmounting the obstacle. With practice, you'll soon be able to spot any of these obstacles as soon as it rears its head, and take swift action to correct the situation. Your reward? A high-performing team that achieves its mission and produces valuable business results for your organization.

Anne Donnellon, Mentor

Professor Anne Donnellon of the F.W. Olin Graduate School of Business at Babson College has been researching, consulting, and teaching about teams inside organizations for more than a decade. She is the author of *Team Talk: The Power of Language in Team Dynamics* (Harvard Business School Press) and is the content expert for *Teams That Work* from the award-winning Interactive Manager Series by Harvard Business School Publishing. She has also written several Harvard Business School cases, two of which focus on cross-functional teams: "Medisys Corp: The IntensCare Product Development Team" and "Mod IV Product Development Team."

Managing Teams: The Basics

Keeping Your
Team on Track

I magine that you're leading a team. Things have gone well so far: the members are working well together; the team is progressing toward its objectives. Suddenly, however, problems arise. Perhaps two members get embroiled in a personal conflict, or the team as a whole can't seem to make decisions. Maybe communication within the team becomes unproductive—some members aren't contributing to discussions, while others are interrupting one another frequently.

Whatever the problem, you must take action if you want your team to succeed. To keep your team on target, you must constantly evaluate its process (how the team is achieving its results) and make necessary midcourse corrections. You also have to understand the kinds of internal obstacles that can derail a team and develop techniques to remove those obstacles.

Evaluating the team's process

Team process is the way in which the team is achieving its results—such as how well members are resolving conflicts, cultivating positive interpersonal relationships, sharing information, and managing project budgets and schedules.

When a team encounters internal obstacles, an evaluation of its process becomes particularly crucial. There are several means to do this. The table "Methods for evaluating team process" provides some examples.

TABLE 1

Methods for evaluating team process

Method	Definition	Example
Benchmarking	The team compares its process to that of other, similar teams in the company.	A team charged with improving customer service compares the level of trust and member participation in weekly meetings in a team in another department.
Outside observer	An external consultant observes the team and objectively evaluates its process.	A team developing an employee survey hires a consultant to analyze the quality of its interpersonal relationships. The consultant draws on his or her knowledge of other teams and team dynamics to suggest changes.
Ongoing team discussions	Team members engage in regular, informal discussions to assess their own process.	A team evaluating new marketing databases meets weekly to discuss its progress, including how well the team is managing deadlines, meeting budget goals, and solving problems.
Project debriefing sessions	After the team completes a task, members meet to identify what went well and what didn't.	A team designing a new self-service employee benefits system meets after completing the Web site for the project. Members discuss how well the team learned new skills and collaborated while creating the site.

To evaluate your team's process, you may also find it helpful to have members provide feedback for one another. The most constructive criticism often comes from other team members because they are most familiar with each other's work. But proceed gently here: some team members may feel uncomfortable evaluating their peers. To get started, try having everyone share his or her opinion of how effective the team has been and what it needs to do to improve. If there is a general consensus about these issues, move on to feedback about individual members—have each person begin with a self-assessment. Be prepared to handle conflict, anger, or hurt feelings when members start evaluating each other.

Tip: Make sure you provide feedback at regular intervals throughout the project. This can help you correct problems as soon as you diagnose them. Also conduct a debriefing session after a project is completed. This can help your team take stock of what went well and what didn't, and identify lessons to apply to future projects.

Understanding common obstacles

Teams can run into numerous internal obstacles as they work toward their objectives. The table "Common obstacles for teams" shows some of the more common problems and provides examples of behaviors that characterize each of them.

TABLE 2

Common obstacles for teams

Problem	Characteristic behaviors
Lack of team identity	• The team's goals conflict with members' personal goals. • Team members lack commitment to goals and don't make significant effort. • Members don't feel accountable to one another. • The team suffers from poor collaboration, information sharing, and joint decision making.
Low participation	• Team members fail to complete assignments. • There's poor attendance at team meetings. • There's low energy during meetings. • Team members are reviewing e-mail or doing other work during meetings.
Poor communication	• Members interrupt or talk over one another. • Some members remain silent during meetings. • People allude to problems but don't formally address them. • Everyone nods in agreement when a course of action is proposed, but it's just a false consensus; no one follows up on the agreed-on decision.
Ineffective team leadership	• Team members contribute few ideas. • They can't seem to define a vision for the team. • The team leader fails to delegate. • The leader doesn't seem to know how to represent multiple constituencies.
Destructive conflict	• Arguments break out frequently. • Team members don't provide emotional support for one another. • People make aggressive gestures, such as leaving meetings or threatening to quit the team. • Tensions and personal critiques or attacks persist.

(continued)

TABLE 2 (continued)

Problem	Characteristic behaviors
Groupthink	• Team members are unwilling or unable to consider alternative ideas. • There's a lack of debate over ideas. • Critical thinking is treated as a roadblock to team progress. • Members demonstrate an overriding desire for team agreement and unity.
Absence of creativity	• Members seem unable to generate fresh ideas and perspectives beyond the prevailing wisdom or established ways of doing things. • Members regularly use the established ways as reasons that new ideas won't work. • People are unwilling to ask questions or be curious and playful. • Members don't seem to know how to turn unexpected events into opportunities.
Ineffective decision making	• Members adhere rigidly to their positions during decision making. • Arguments erupt frequently and don't produce any useful new information. • Decisions are constantly being revisited.

In the sections that follow, we'll take a closer look at each of these eight common obstacles to team performance. We'll consider why each obstacle is so dangerous and examine potent strategies for removing the obstacles. Let's start with lack of team identity.

Obstacle 1: Lack of Team Identity

Team identity is the members' sense that they share a bond and a purpose. This sense is critical for any team's success. To strengthen team identity, first understand why it's so crucial.

Appreciating why team identity is crucial

Team identity is critical for several reasons. For one thing, it encourages mutual accountability for results. When team members see that together they are accountable for producing desired outcomes, they work hard to deliver their contributions and efforts on time and as promised so as not to hold up teammates. They also help teammates who are struggling or falling behind. Poor performers feel motivated to do better. And members drop the "I did my share" attitude that weakens performance. In fact, some experts view mutual accountability as the single most important contributor to team performance.

Team identity also evokes commitment and effort. It creates the sense that members share a common interest in the team's success. With team identity, people become more willing to collaborate, share information, make a greater effort, make joint decisions, and put team goals ahead of personal goals.

Simply put, a strong team identity helps keep teams on target.

What Would YOU Do?

Fresh Troubles at Fresh Face, Inc.

ESMERALDA HAS RECENTLY tasked her team with designing a marketing campaign for a new line of environmentally responsible cosmetics at Fresh Face, Inc. For the past few months, Esmeralda has worked hard to build trust and commitment in her group. Everything had been going smoothly until Joseph, a designer hired to work specifically on the campaign's printed brochures, joined the team.

One day, Esmeralda overheard several team members talking, and one of them suggested to the other that Joseph "doesn't know what he's doing." The other added, "He sure doesn't seem to know how to collaborate." Later that week, Esmeralda arrived at a "team" lunch in the break room to find that no one had told Joseph about the lunch: he was still in his cubicle, working.

Esmeralda doesn't understand. Joseph is extremely competent and shows real passion for his work. She is shocked and disappointed to see her team excluding him. She rubs her chin and wonders how to handle the situation.

What would YOU do? The mentor will suggest a solution in *What You COULD Do*.

Understanding causes of weak team identity

In addition to understanding why team identity is so important, it's also helpful to know what causes weakness in a team's identity. Experts have proposed several causes:

- **Newness of the team.** It's natural for new teams to suffer from some lack of identity. A feeling of team identity builds as people have opportunities to interact, discuss a common goal, or join forces in attacking a problem.

- **Newly introduced members.** When new members join the team after the work has begun, team identity can suffer if newcomers introduce new ways of thinking, if they don't operate in the same way as others, or if they are made to feel like outsiders.

- **Diversity of members.** The very differences that give a team its potential for high performance can sometimes make it difficult for members to develop a sense of team identity. Why? Differing assumptions, cultural backgrounds, and ways of working and thinking can lead to misunderstandings or tensions among members. For example, on a research and development team comprising members from three different nations, people from a country in which formality is valued might bristle if their counterparts from another nation address them in casual terms.

A successful team is a group of many hands but of one mind.
—Bill Bethel

Strengthening team identity

As a team leader, you *can*—and should—take steps to strengthen team identity while also maintaining members' valuable differences. But how can you achieve this? The following techniques can help:

- **Reiterate the team's common goals.** Frequently revisit the team's shared goals and purpose to remind people that the work they are doing is important—not just to the team, but to the organization as well.

- **Encourage collaborative work.** Find as many opportunities as possible to get people working together. Nothing builds team identity like collaborating side by side on a challenge.

- **Strengthen bonding.** Create opportunities for members to know each other; for example, through lunches in the team room, an offsite outing, or other events. Stereotypes such as "those engineers are hard to work with" will gradually disappear.

- **Implant a sense of urgency.** When team members feel that their work is crucial, they try harder to reach goals and feel compelled to join together to meet the challenge at hand. To create a sense of urgency, impress on the team how their work will solve a serious problem or benefit the company. For instance, "This product we're developing is going to help us become the market leader and leave our competitors far behind."

- **Recognize the value of team differences.** Publicly acknowledge the value of differences among team members, and explain how those differences serve the team's common goal. For example, two members who bring different perspectives on customers' needs can stimulate other members to come up with creative ideas for developing innovative products.

- **Create engaging activities.** Encourage members to take part in activities they find interesting and valuable, such as defining a team charter, developing a schedule for completing a major task, or meeting with clients. Such activities will keep them focused on the team's objectives.

- **Recruit team members selectively.** When assembling your team or bringing in additional team members, look for people who see the team's goals as important and worthwhile. These individuals will be predisposed to achieve the goals rather than focus on differences within the team.

- **Integrate newcomers.** Be particularly attentive to team identity when new members join the team after work has commenced. Newcomers are bound to feel like outsiders at first. Quickly engage them in team projects so that they feel welcome and integrated into the group. If appropriate, hold a welcome lunch or other small social event to mark a new member's arrival.

- **Acknowledge team members' skills.** Find opportunities to publicly acknowledge and express appreciation for the skills and contributions of individual team members. And explain how their efforts have helped the team make progress toward its goals. This will make team members feel valued and appreciated, and strengthen their commitment to the group.

- **Use concrete symbols.** Consider using emblems such as team T-shirts or hats to help people identify with the team and its values.

What You COULD Do.

Remember Esmeralda's concerns about how her team has been excluding Joseph?

Here's what the mentor suggests:

Esmeralda needs to resolve this situation quickly if she hopes to keep her team on target. A top priority is to work with the team as a whole on a project so she can assess Joseph and the others, as well as signal how important collaboration is to the team's goals. Lending Joseph some of her own prestige can help motivate others to integrate him more fully into the team. She might also meet individually with all team members—including Joseph—to find out how things are going. Moreover, she should ask questions and allow team members to voice their opinions without interruptions. Above all, she should actively listen to what's being said. By better understanding the concerns of the group, she will, in turn, get to the root causes of the problem. Depending on what she hears, Esmeralda might want to follow up again with certain members of the team.

Obstacle 2: Low Participation

A team can't succeed if some or all of its members don't participate wholeheartedly in its work, meetings, and social events. With low participation, the team loses out on the fresh ideas, knowledge, skills, and other important strengths that individual members bring to the team's work. For this reason, it's important to know when your team is suffering from low participation and to take immediate steps to correct the problem.

Detecting low participation

How do you detect low participation in your team? Watch for members' failure to complete assignments, as well as poor attendance at team meetings and get-togethers aimed at celebrating achievement of major milestones. During meetings, observe team members and gauge their energy levels. Lackluster energy and attention are additional symptoms of poor participation.

Confirming expectations about participation

When you formed your team, did you establish rules for participation—such as the following?

- "Members must attend every meeting and arrive at meetings on time."

- "We agree to complete all assignments that we signed up for."

- "Each of us is accountable to one another for coming to meetings prepared."

If you did establish such norms, revisit them in a team meeting and ask members whether they still agree on the rules. If so, reiterate the need for these norms: they ensure broad participation across the entire team. Acknowledge that outside pressures and demanding schedules can sometimes make it hard for people to participate in the team as fully as they should. But stress the importance of participation. It can also be informative to ask why people are not participating as was agreed.

If team members no longer believe that certain participation norms are valuable, ask why. If necessary, create new norms—but ensure that they specifically encourage participation. And most important, if participation norms are not currently in place, consider creating some immediately.

Enabling members to meet expectations

If team members are having difficulty fulfilling agreed-on expectations about participation, find out why and then develop solutions to make the situation better. For example, suppose some members of your team have been coming to meetings unprepared. Develop ways to ensure that people are better prepared. These might include establishing several new rules, such as:

- All reading materials for meetings should be distributed to team members at least three days before the meeting.

- The person who distributes reading materials before a meeting should include a note explaining what readers are expected to do with the material—for instance, "For your information only," "To make a decision on the product prototype," "To generate suggestions for new features in the information technology system we're considering."

Solutions might also include new processes. For instance, if people are having trouble completing assignments, trace the events that led up to the delays (such as bottlenecks). Then identify ways to redistribute work among team members so that bottlenecks are then eliminated.

Asking for explanations

At times, simply asking people why they're having trouble participating can reveal valuable information you can then use to develop solutions. Asking for explanations can also uncover problems that you and other team members haven't been aware of.

For example, suppose that Eric, a member of a project team you're leading, has been reticent during meetings. In this case, you might take Eric aside and say, "I've noticed that you've been pretty quiet during our weekly meetings, and I'm concerned that we're missing out on your ideas for this project. What's going on?"

Eric responds, "I'm feeling overloaded. My boss asked me to submit a project two weeks earlier than planned. I've had to work overtime to meet that deadline and still fulfill my commitments to this team. I've been exhausted."

Your exchange with Eric has uncovered information that may suggest helpful changes. For instance, if it turns out that Eric expects his regular job responsibilities to be unusually demanding for the next two weeks, you might consider asking another team member to take over part of his team-related tasks for that period of time. Once Eric's regular job is back under control, he can then resume his team commitments. Use this as an example of how the team depends on full participation and how the team can adjust to team members' needs when such realities are shared openly.

Assessing member/task fit

In some cases, low participation stems from a poor fit between team members and the tasks they've been assigned or have agreed to take on. To illustrate, suppose you're leading a team charged with developing an employee benefits survey. You've assigned Maha the task of creating the survey because she has a strong writing background. As the project unfolds, it turns out that Maha lacks the design skills needed to complete the survey. Thus, she has been having difficulty meeting interim deadlines.

In such cases, it's vital to identify what's causing the poor fit and take steps to address it. For instance, you could work out a plan that would enable Maha to work with an outside designer who could suggest some design templates. Or you could consider asking Maha to write the survey and shift the survey's design to a person more experienced in this area.

Obstacle 3: Poor Communication

I n addition to lack of team identity and low participation, poor communication can seriously derail a team, preventing it from achieving its goals and fulfilling its purpose. Let's take a closer look at the costs of poor communication and explore ideas for how you can enhance your team members' communication skills.

Understanding the costs of poor communication

When team members communicate poorly, a team can suffer a number of negative consequences. Troubled communication can cause interpersonal conflict in the form of personal attacks, sarcasm, and arguing. It can also prompt team members to interrupt or talk over one another during meetings, to remain silent, or to hint at problems while never formally addressing them.

Perhaps the most destructive consequence of poor communication for teams is difficulty in reaching an informed decision. When team members withhold information or attack one another's ideas, the ability to generate creative solutions to problems is stifled, and bad decisions result.

Enhancing team members' communication skills

Teams can't work toward their goals if members don't communicate constructively. If you've diagnosed communication problems in your team, you need to take action quickly. The following measures can help:

- **Focus on behavior, not character.** Encourage team members to express their anger or frustration in terms of other people's behavior, rather than their personal character. In addition, remind people to use "I" language rather than "you" language. With "I" language, people describe the impact of another person's behavior on them.

  For instance, suppose Sue is angry with Timothy for missing a deadline. In this case, it's more productive for her to say, "When you missed the deadline, I ended up finishing my part of the project late." If instead she had told Timothy, "You clearly aren't committed to this project," he would almost certainly feel that she was attacking his character—and become defensive in response.

- **Create rules for contentious discussion.** Acknowledge to your team that contentious conversations will almost inevitably occur as members work out solutions to problems, make decisions, and explore ideas. The question isn't *whether* contentiousness will arise, but rather *how* your team will deal with it when it does take place.

  Work with your team to define rules about how to have a contentious discussion. Whenever necessary, revisit the rules and remind people to follow them. The rules that teams develop vary from team to team, but some examples might include the following: "Wait for another person to finish speaking before jumping into the conversation." "Acknowledge the value of another person's idea, even if you don't agree with it." "If you disagree with someone, explain the reasons behind your position."

- **Solicit team members' views.** In any team, it's common for some people to dominate discussions and others to remain quiet. The longer the team works together, the more entrenched members become in these roles—and the more the team loses out on valuable input from all members. Take steps to ensure that *all* members contribute their views and ideas during team discussions and meetings. Again, establishing communication norms can help.

  For example, if you notice someone remaining silent during a discussion, invite him or her to provide input. Point out that "during any discussion, each team member must provide input one at a time—no matter how brief" or "we will examine all opposing points of view."

- **Use meeting time wisely.** Insist that everyone be familiar with the agenda and any required reading materials before coming to a team meeting. During meetings, focus on problem solving rather than information sharing. If the discussion strays, steer it back to items on the meeting agenda. And discuss new business at the end of the meeting. See "Steps for keeping team meetings on the right track" for more information.

- **Focus attention on team goals.** Talking about goals helps to focus team communication and direct people's attention away from interpersonal conflicts or other distractions. To improve communication, revisit the team's initial purpose periodically. And write frequent progress reports to distribute to all team members. When people see their progress in writing, they'll be able to communicate about the team's effort in a focused way.

Steps for keeping team meetings on the right track

1. **Follow a predetermined agenda that's been distributed to participants ahead of time.** If each participant knows in advance what will be discussed, everyone will be more likely to stick to the topics at hand. Allocate time allotments by the priority of the issue.
2. **Open the meeting by stating its purpose and objectives.** Explain how the meeting's purpose relates to the team's overall goals and what you hope to accomplish through the meeting.
3. **Let everyone have a say.** All opinions, suggestions, and constructive criticism should be welcome. Show support for the expression of views with which you may disagree. Tell members that they will not be censured for an unpopular opinion, as long as they're trying to accomplish the team's goals. Try to encourage others to explore such opinions instead of dismissing them out of hand. It can be helpful to give people time limits for expression of their views. Careful time management by the leader is critical.
4. **Gain closure on each issue.** Using the decision-making method that team members have agreed to (majority rule, consensus,

small group, or leader with input), ensure that each issue up for decision is resolved during the meeting.

5. **Leave time at the end of each meeting for new business or unscheduled items.** By carving out time for new business or unscheduled items at the end of the meeting, you help participants stay focused on the agenda during the early part of the meeting.

6. **End the meeting with an action and communication plan.** A good action and communication plan specifies *what* got decided at the meeting and what tasks need to be done as a result of the meeting, *who* has responsibility for those tasks, and *when* the tasks must be completed.

7. **Distribute the plan.** Send the action and communication plan to all meeting participants and to people who weren't at the meeting but need to be informed of the outcome.

Obstacle 4:
Ineffective Team
Leadership

If you've noticed difficulties with identity, participation, and communication in your team, it may be time to consider whether your team is suffering from another obstacle to success: ineffective team leadership. Not surprisingly, that possibility is a tough one for team leaders to acknowledge and grapple with. After all, few people find it easy to admit that they're perhaps not leading their team as well as they should.

But avoiding this issue won't help you *or* your team deliver top-notch performance. So let's dig into this issue, with the goal of honestly assessing your team's leadership and committing to being the best leader possible.

Recognizing the signs of poor leadership

How can you discern if you or another team leader is providing less-than-stellar leadership? Look for these symptoms:

- Team member participation is low; people aren't contributing ideas and opinions during meetings and decision-making sessions.

- People are unable to explain why the team's work or project is important to the company and how it will benefit the organization.

- The team leader is taking on more responsibilities than the team members are.

- Conflict is persistent, and decisions do not get made.

- Team members feel that their leader is representing only one of many constituencies; for example, that he or she is favoring members with technical expertise over those with other skills or backgrounds.

If you see any of these things happening, it's time to step back and examine how you're leading your team—and make some changes to provide more effective leadership. A helpful first step is to understand the root causes of poor leadership in a team.

You get the best out of others when you give the best of yourself.
—Harry Firestone

Identifying the root causes

What causes a team leader to be ineffective? In some cases, a novice team leader may have difficulty making the transition into the team leader role. Even experienced managers find that team leadership is challenging. The transition becomes especially difficult if the team leader has acted only as an individual contributor in the past. Individual contributors are used to handling work themselves rather than managing others' work. If they refuse to delegate, they prevent their team from leveraging the skills and expertise of all its members.

Team leadership problems may stem from several other tendencies as well. For example, because many team leaders are managers, they may continue to act like traditional bosses while leading their teams. In their view, "Leaders tell their teams what to do and how to do it." But team members need some degree of autonomy if the team as a whole is to succeed.

In other cases, a team leader erroneously believes that he or she has "empowered" the team and therefore can take a hands-off approach. This doesn't work either, because teams also need some degree of guidance.

In addition to mastering the art of delegation, team leaders must also learn to balance "bossing" with "empowering."

Balancing bossing with empowering

Experts agree that team leaders must maintain a *balance* between being a boss and empowering team members. How to strike this balance? First, spell out your team's objectives to enable members to focus on their goals and make any needed midcourse corrections as they work toward achieving those goals. *But at the same time,* let team members decide *how* to achieve the objectives you've defined. Team members will act as a team only if they have real autonomy and a sense of mutual accountability and ownership of their work.

Second, if you're leading a team and you see symptoms of poor leadership, take an honest look at yourself. Ask whether you're being too much of a boss, or taking too much of a hands-off approach to your team. Consider getting some coaching to identify ways to correct the boss/empowerment balance in your leadership style. Or ask the team sponsor for his or her guidance.

Third, tapping into senior management's vision can also help. Keep company leadership apprised of your team's progress to ensure that the team is moving in a direction consistent with the larger vision. Communicate frequently with senior leadership to see if there have been any changes to company-level strategies or goals that your team needs to know about. And ask senior management for help if you need it. For example, if corporate strategy has changed and your team needs additional skills to help carry out the strategy, seek approval for any needed training.

See "Tips for balancing bossing with empowering" for additional ideas.

Tips for balancing bossing with empowering

- Clarify the team's objectives or the "what," but leave it up to team members to decide what steps they will take to achieve those objectives (the "how").
- Identify informal leaders within your team by assessing their behavior and the degree of deference they receive from others.
- Ensure that informal leaders understand the team's goals, know why those goals are important, and accept those goals as their own.
- Cultivate positive relationships with informal leaders on your team, and use those relationships to communicate the big picture to others.
- Encourage team members to share and rotate leadership among themselves. For example, give people ample opportunities to head up ad hoc task forces, arrange offsite meetings, and so on.

- Hold team members accountable for results and the quality of team processes.
- Display passionate commitment to the team's mission to encourage the same among team members.

Taking action when you're not the leader

What if you're a member of a team led by someone else, and you suspect that the leader is the source of the team's problems? This situation raises some delicate issues. But there *are* several steps you can take to address the problem. Consider these guidelines:

- **Meet with the team leader to discuss perceived deficiencies.** Follow productive communication guidelines by using "I" language and describing the impact that the leader's behavior is having on the team. For example, "I noticed that only two people offered ideas during the last meeting. I think we may not be exploring enough alternatives, and I'm worried that the team won't make the best decision. Is there something we could do to solicit contributions from more team members?"

- **Volunteer to share the workload.** By volunteering, you may boost your chances of encouraging your team's leader to delegate more. Delegating is essential for any team because it enables the leader to leverage the blend of skills, experience, and ideas that the team's members bring to the work.

- **Consult with the team sponsor.** If you've concluded that a leadership problem is unresolvable through direct communication with your team's leader, bring the problem to the team sponsor—the manager or executive who has a stake in the outcome of the project and is accountable for the team's performance. Get his or her opinions about next steps.

Team leaders have a complex set of responsibilities to fulfill, so it's not surprising that they frequently face difficulties. The best leaders, however, know when it's time to reassess their skills or adjust their approach. And the best team members know when and how to help their leader stay on the right track.

Obstacle 5:
Destructive Conflict

Destructive conflict is another common obstacle a team may encounter as it begins its work. Conflicts within a team can take numerous forms—from tensions and arguments to an unwillingness to support others or passive-aggressive behavior. Left unresolved, such conflicts can destroy a team's ability to make progress toward its goals.

How can you avoid this scenario and bring a conflict to resolution? Experts recommend the following four-step process:

1. Define the root cause of the conflict.

2. Encourage active listening.

3. Negotiate a resolution.

4. Remind team members to forgive.

Next, we'll examine each of these steps.

Defining the root cause of the conflict

When conflict arises in your team, ask yourself the following questions:

- "Why are team members arguing with each other?"

- "Is there a deeper personality conflict here?"

- "Are there organizational causes of this conflict?"

- "Is this a recurring pattern?"

- "Why is one member being stubborn?"

- "Why does one member always insist on getting his or her way?"

- "Is the cause of this conflict a behavior? A clash of opinions? A situation?"

Your answers to these questions will help you uncover the conflict's root cause—whether it's a behavior, a disagreement over ideas, or something about the situation (such as a lack of resources or a change in the scope of the team's project).

By understanding the root cause, you can generate ideas for negotiating a resolution to the conflict. For instance, if the conflict is caused by a personality clash, the resolution might take the form of helping the two combatants learn to communicate better with one another and practice more respectful dialogue when they disagree on something. If the conflict is caused by a situation, you and your team can work out ways to address the problem; for example, finding sources of additional needed resources or renegotiating a project's scope.

Tip: When diagnosing the root cause of a conflict, ask "What really seems to be a stake for those involved in the conflict?" Often what seems to be a clash of personalities is really a conflict born of organizational roles or team design flaws. So, push yourself to look more deeply at the possible causes of conflict.

Encouraging active listening

As you and your team discuss ways to negotiate a resolution to a conflict, it's vital that all members become active listeners. That is, they must be able to:

- **Restate points** made by a speaker to demonstrate that they've understood what the speaker is saying.

- **Control behavior** that suggests a lack of interest in the speaker; for instance, doodling, fidgeting, interrupting, or checking e-mail while someone else is talking.

- **Ask questions** that encourage a speaker to expand on his or her points with further information or lines of reasoning.

- **Refer back** to points made earlier and build on those ideas.

- **Ask speakers** to explain the reasons behind their opinions.

"No interrupting" is an especially crucial rule for active listening. If necessary, remind team members that each person has the right to offer his or her ideas and solutions to problems without interruption. Point out that each person should be able to finish his or her thoughts even if one or more other team members disagree. Of course, managing team members who talk too long is also critical, so avoid using this rule unless your team really needs it.

Explain, too, that there often isn't just one right answer to a conflict or problem. A team needs to consider a broad range of possible solutions before feeling confident that it has selected the best one. In fact, one of the reasons a team is created is to get varying opinions on how to solve problems. Allowing people with different perspectives and skills to voice their ideas without interruption is one good way to gather those opinions.

Finally, acknowledge the presence of painful feelings, such as anger and frustration. Explain that holding in anger will only lead to resentment. Letting everyone share his or her frustrations in a constructive way will let the team move on to solutions.

Negotiating a resolution

Once you understand the root cause of the conflict, avoid dictating a resolution. Instead, negotiate a solution that everyone involved can live with. Point out the importance of agreeing to disagree on certain issues. Remind people that if one member bullies the rest of the team into accepting his or her viewpoint, the rest of the members will resent that person and not support the decision.

Encourage members to find common ground and explore new possibilities. For example, suppose two team members are arguing over the best way to complete a report on time. Don't allow the team to "gang up" on a member who has a different idea. Ensure that each member feels safe in offering a divergent opinion. In this case, you might say, "You both want the same result here—a report finished on time. But you're recommending different ways to get there. Let's discuss the pros and cons of the two different approaches you're arguing over. And let's bring some additional alternatives into the picture. That way, we'll stand a better chance of selecting the best solution."

Tip: Don't take sides in a conflict within your team. Instead, *moderate* the discussion. Consider scripting what you plan to say, and anticipating how others will respond.

Reminding team members to forgive

Once your team has negotiated a resolution to a conflict, remind people to forgive one another for any hurt feelings or damaged egos. Point out that forgiveness is not a sign of weakness or of a propensity to "give in." Rather, it enables people to let go of any anger left over from a conflict, and it prevents the anger from poisoning future encounters among team members.

Tip: Encourage forgiveness by practicing forgiveness yourself. Don't hold a grudge. Don't harbor ill will after a conflict has been resolved. And remember to apologize when you've done something wrong.

"Strategies for making the most of conflict" offers additional suggestions for surmounting this common barrier to team progress.

Strategies for making the most of conflict

- Encourage team members to listen to one another and consider different viewpoints—perhaps by inviting two people to switch positions and argue for the side they previously opposed.
- Make it clear that you *want* contentious issues aired, and that *anyone* can point out an issue without retribution.
- Even if only one person thinks there's a problem that needs discussing, acknowledge the issue that he or she has raised.
- Remind people of the norms the team has agreed on for how members treat each other.
- Encourage members who raise concerns to describe the issue as specifically as possible.
- Keep the discussion impersonal by discussing *what* is impeding progress, not who is "to blame."
- If the issue involves a team member's behavior, encourage the person who identified the problem to explain how the behavior affects him or her, rather than making assumptions about what's motivating the behavior.
- End the discussion with concrete suggestions for improvement, if not a solution to the problem.
- If the conversation ends up going nowhere because the subject at hand is too sensitive, consider adjourning the discussion until a specified later date so that people can cool down.
- Consider bringing in a facilitator for especially heated conversations.

Obstacle 6:
"Groupthink"

As a team leader, you of course want your group to be close-knit and feel a strong sense of team identity. Without that cohesiveness, the team can't make decisions, solve problems, and work toward its goals. But *too* much of this good thing can cause your close-knit team to fall victim to a pattern of thought called groupthink. And the more close-knit the team is, the higher the risk.

Groupthink is an undesirable condition in which team members think alike to the point where they're unwilling to raise concerns about a project—even though these concerns are legitimate and based on hard data. Groupthink is driven by social pressures, such as individuals' needs to highlight similarities among themselves and suppress differences.

Understanding the dangers of groupthink

To be sure, thinking alike can engender cooperation and help a team focus on goals, make decisions, and follow agreed-on norms of behavior. However, when convergence of opinion becomes extreme, it escalates to groupthink. And that's dangerous to a team for several reasons:

- It curtails critical thinking and debate—two essential ingredients for an effective team.

- The impulse for team agreement and unity takes priority over objectivity, which the team needs to weigh options and make informed decisions.

- As diversity of views gives way to extreme convergence in team members' thinking, people experience an illusion of certitude. They feel that it is no longer necessary for them to consider alternatives.

- Team members who "think otherwise" may be "reeducated" or pushed off the team, worsening the tendency toward groupthink.

Why does groupthink happen? Some experts maintain that opinion within groups tends to converge as members become aware of their peers' opinions. Perhaps owing to a lack of self-confidence or a desire to remain in good standing within the team, members become reluctant to offer viewpoints that are out of step with others.

Recognizing the symptoms

Whatever the cause of groupthink, you need to guard against it in your team—and take active steps to discourage it. Your first move? Know the symptoms of groupthink:

- People accept data confirming their view and reject data that opposes it.

- Members neglect to consider alternatives when making decisions.

What Would YOU Do?

Maximizing Team Communication at MaxGlobal

MIGUEL HEADS the benefits administration group within MaxGlobal's human resources department. Some months ago, his team was tasked with a challenging project: evaluating potential new benefits programs and then selecting and implementing the most promising one.

The team has made major strides on the project. However, it has also encountered some significant challenges that have created tension among team members. At several recent meetings, the discussion has taken an awkward, negative turn. In Miguel's view, members aren't "talking like a team" as much as they used to. In fact, many of them are not talking at all, and some are not even attending all the meetings. He's concerned that if the tension increases, it will destroy the group's morale and productivity.

One night, as he's talking with a former colleague about the problem, he brings up the subject. "I'm not sure how to improve the way my team members are communicating," he says. "Should I encourage everyone to contribute by asking their opinions during meetings? Maybe I should start meetings by sharing more information. It could serve as fodder for more conversation. I've also thought about designating one of the members as a devil's advocate for whenever a major debate breaks out. I can see several possible solutions to this situation. I guess I just need to focus on the one or two best ones."

What would YOU do? The mentor will suggest a solution in *What You COULD Do*.

- People discount or even demonize individuals whose views are out of step with those of the majority.

- The pressure for a rapid decision, perhaps in the interest of efficiency or costs of delay, cuts off debate.

- An illusion of invulnerability prevails in the team.

- Members protect or insulate the team leader from contradictory evidence.

If you see any of these things happening in *your* team, take action to combat groupthink.

Combating groupthink

The best antidote to groupthink is a diversity of thoughtful ideas. To welcome such ideas into your team, issue early cautions about groupthink. As you form your team and launch the team project, caution members about the nature and dangers of groupthink. Explain that as the team becomes more close-knit, the risk of groupthink will rise. Invite people to offer ideas for preventing groupthink. Distribute a list of the symptoms of groupthink, and ask members to watch for them as the team moves forward in its work.

Also, actively seek objectivity. Empower a few individuals on your team who are smart and well regarded to objectively represent dissenting ideas and data. Have this special group examine and report back on every one of the team's key assumptions.

Finally, appoint a respected and qualified team member to play the role of a devil's advocate—someone who challenges the prevailing point of view. Charge this person with challenging the assumptions and conclusions of the majority. Or as suggested earlier, rotate this responsibility within the team, so everyone gains the experience of acting as a legitimate devil's advocate.

?What You COULD Do.

Remember Miguel's question about how best to improve communication in his team?

Here's what the mentor suggests:

Miguel should definitely expect all team members to contribute their opinions during meetings. He might need to do some fact-finding with individuals to learn why there isn't more exchange of views. In the meeting, he can restate his expectations about active and full participation. By voicing what they think of a proposal or idea, team members stay involved in the team's conversational process. Miguel can further encourage participation by stopping the free flow of conversation occasionally, going around the table, and inviting the team members, one by one, to "add their two cents." People will feel more involved, as well as benefit from one another's opinions.

His idea about designating a team member as a devil's advocate during major debates is also a good one. A devil's advocate can stimulate members to reexamine their perspectives. Rotating this responsibility gives everyone practice in how to stimulate more creative or critical thinking. This process encourages a group to deliberately explore opposing points of view. It also helps the team avoid groupthink.

Providing more information during meetings to serve as conversational fodder would not be the wisest course of action. Sharing more information—especially details that can be distributed to everyone before the meeting—only wastes valuable meeting time. Instead, everyone should stay focused on solving problems during meetings. By distributing detailed information a day or so before the meeting, Miguel can help the group maintain focus.

Obstacle 7: Absence of Creativity

reativity—the ability to approach a problem in an original and flexible way—is another important element in most team-based work. Creativity helps team members generate fresh perspectives, spot opportunities that they hadn't anticipated, and develop innovative solutions to problems. Without creativity, a team can't perform at its best.

As the leader of your team, you can do several things to foster creativity among team members. These include promoting diversity of styles and skills, balancing the paradoxical characteristics of your team, and moving team members back and forth as needed between divergent and convergent thinking.

Promoting diversity of thinking styles and technical skills

Teams can achieve greater creative output than individuals working alone because they bring a broader range of competencies, insights, experiences, and energy to the effort. But to reap that creative output, groups must have the right composition of thinking styles and technical skills. In most cases, that means a *diversity* of styles and skills.

This variety has several benefits. For one thing, individual differences can produce the creative friction that sparks new ideas. Moreover, diversity of ideas and perspectives guards against people's tendency to converge around just one point of view. Team members explore a wide variety of viewpoints and ideas, which increases the chances that they'll arrive at the best possible course of action for their work.

Team leaders thus need to carefully consider how teams are staffed. In assembling your team and bringing in any new members after the work has begun, strive to build diversity of thinking styles and technical skills into the team's composition. For instance, ask yourself, "Have I assembled a team of people who tackle problems in different ways and from different angles? Do we have in our group all the technical skills related to the work at hand and needed to accomplish our mission? What about other important skills—such as the ability to tolerate conflict and to collaboratively develop solutions?"

Balancing paradoxical characteristics

To function effectively, a team needs a balance of several different qualities. For example:

- It needs skilled expertise *and* fresh, inexperienced perspectives. To strike this balance, bring in outsiders to augment the more seasoned members.

- It must work within the confines of real business needs *while also* having the latitude to determine how it will meet those needs. To achieve this balance, make business needs clear while letting your team make decisions about how to reach its goals.

- It can benefit from both professionalism *and* playfulness. Creativity thrives on playfulness, but business must be conducted professionally. To maintain this balance, provide time and space for play, but clarify the appropriate times and places.

- It must plan projects carefully *while also* improvising when projects inevitably don't go as planned. To balance planning with improvisation, encourage team members to look for ways to turn unexpected events into opportunities. And keep plans flexible enough to incorporate new ideas.

Moving from divergent to convergent thinking

Your team's creativity stems from two types of thinking:

- **Divergent thinking**—seeing and doing things in a range of nontraditional ways, and viewing familiar things from a variety of new angles.

- **Convergent thinking**—channeling the results of divergent thinking into concrete proposals for action.

To generate the *most* creativity, a team needs to engage first in divergent thinking and then in convergent thinking. The harder of these is divergent thinking, but making the transition to convergent thinking once you have people generating divergent ideas can also be challenging.

During *divergent* thinking, team members ask questions that haven't been asked before, analyze problems and situations from different perspectives, and make connections among facts or events that others have missed. Divergent thinking generates a wide variety of options that in turn trigger new insights and ideas.

Once the team has completed its divergent-thinking sessions, it moves to *convergent* thinking. Convergent thinking answers the question: "Are the insights we've generated valuable?" Through convergent thinking, team members evaluate the ideas generated by divergent thinking to determine which are genuinely novel—and which are worth pursuing.

Convergence sets limits, narrowing the field of solutions within a given set of constraints. How do you determine those constraints? Your company's culture, mission, priorities, and high-level context for the team's project all contribute to the answer. They help you rule out options that lie beyond the scope of your project. But you can facilitate this process by asking specific questions.

For example, suppose your team is developing a new product. Through divergent thinking, team members have generated a wide range of ideas for features for the product. In this case, you might ask:

- "Which features are essential from the customer's point of view?"

- "What are the cost constraints? Which of the features we've been considering would fit within those constraints?"

- "How soon must the project be completed? Which of our ideas for features can we implement within that time line?"

Your team's responses to these questions will help you weed out ideas that aren't practical for one reason or another, and focus in on the ones that are.

Obstacle 8: Ineffective Decision Making

Have you ever found yourself in the following situation? You're leading a team and members are discussing an important decision during a meeting. To your dismay, the conversation is going nowhere; people are rigidly adhering to their positions and unable to reach agreement. Despite repeated arguments, no one has provided any new information to move the decision-making process forward. Worse, in two preceding meetings, you've seen your team get into this same dead-end situation.

Somehow, your team is "stuck" in the decision-making process. You know that you need to take action. After all, a team that can't agree on decisions wastes a lot of time or ends up arriving at choices that team members do not, and probably will not, wholeheartedly support. Either way, it's bad news for the team.

Next, you'll find several potent strategies for helping your team "get unstuck" in its decision making.

Agreeing on a decision-making approach

When you first assembled your team, you probably helped members agree on *who* would make team decisions and *how* decision making would unfold.

You may have selected one of these four common decision-making methods:

- **Majority rule**. Members discuss the decision and then vote. The team adopts the choice that receives more than 50 percent of the votes.

- **Consensus**. Every member must agree to adopt a proposed decision. If consensus is impossible, new alternatives are developed and presented for evaluation.

- **Small group**. A subset of individuals with relevant experience and skills make specific decisions.

- **Leader input**. You, as the team leader, gather input from members and use the information to make decisions.

Whatever approach you and your team agreed on, examine the process the team is now using to make decisions. Ask yourself: "Is my team following the agreed-on approach?" If not, remind members of the agreement and take steps to restore adherence to the method you selected.

Of course, sometimes the decision-making method a team selects early on no longer supports the team's work going forward, and decision making unravels. For example, a team initially chose consensus as its decision process, but as the work unfolded, the team had less time to complete its work than it originally assumed. The team found it increasingly difficult to reach consensus under mounting time pressure. Because the consensus method requires more time than other methods, the team opted to change to the small-group method instead.

If conditions have altered for your team, suggesting the need for a new decision-making approach, be willing to consider making a change.

Sharpening decision-making skills

The following techniques can help you sharpen your team members' decision-making skills:

- **Break big decisions into manageable pieces.** If your team gets bogged down in trying to reach agreement on a big decision, break the decision into smaller pieces that may be easier to agree on. For instance, suppose the team is trying to select one of three product designs and can't seem to come to agreement. Focus members' attention on smaller aspects of the decision, for example, by asking: "What are the *most* important features that the new product needs to have?" If members can agree on the answer to that question, they may find it easier to agree on the selection of the product design.

- **Ask what must happen for team members to reach agreement.** For instance, suppose your team is trying to define the scope of a consultant's work. You ask the group, "What needs to happen for you to agree?" Several members respond to your question with comments such as, "We need to understand how this engagement is going to have an impact on our budget" and "We need to know that we can trust the person we select." In this case, such comments may signal that the team could come to agreement if it gathered more information about the consultant's fees or did more research on the consultant's references and previous projects.

- **Remind team members of the costs of "getting stuck."** Point out consequences of unproductive decision making, such as lost time, poor choices, and decisions that many team members won't support. Additional costs are erosion of morale within the team, wasted energy, and diverting the team's attention away from its goals.

Tips and Tools

Tools for Managing Teams

TEAM AUDIT—HOW ARE WE DOING?

Use this audit periodically to gather data from each team member to create a group profile the team can use as a focal point for a discussion about, "How well are we doing as a team?" The discussion provides an opportunity to compare points of view objectively and, if need be, to get back on track and move forward more productively.

Each team member can complete the audit. Individual responses should be kept confidential. Compile the individual responses into a group profile for the team to share in a team meeting.

Team name: | **Date:**

Team goals/Team purpose:

Rate your opinion of the team's effectiveness on the dimensions listed below, with "1" representing an ineffective area in need of improvement to "5" representing an area of effectiveness and strength.

Aspect/ Dimension	Rating: 1 (ineffective) to 5 (effective and strong)					Comments/ Example
	1	2	3	4	5	
Achieving our goals/ purpose						
Improving our process						
Feeling a sense of team identity						
Making decisions						
Communicating						
Resolving conflicts						
Participating in the team						
Generating creative ideas and solutions						
Combating groupthink						
Ensuring effective team leadership						

Comments:

The biggest challenge we face as a team is:

Our greatest strength as a team is:

The one thing I would most like to see the team do is:

TEAM IDENTITY ASSESSMENT

Evaluate how well you are helping your team gain a sense of team identity.

Questions	Yes	No
1. Do you use inclusive pronouns, such as "we," "us," and "our," to underscore that the work being done is a *team* effort?		
2. During meetings, do you refer often to team goals?		
3. When team members disagree, do you ask probing questions to get more information?		
4. Do you encourage collaborative work among your team members?		
5. Do you organize social events to enable team members to get to know one another?		
6. Do you implant a sense of urgency to communicate that the team's work is crucial?		
7. Do you publicly acknowledge the value of differences among team members?		
8. Do you encourage members to take part in work activities they find interesting and valuable?		
9. Do you recruit team members selectively?		
10. Do you integrate newcomers by quickly engaging them in team projects?		
11. Do you recognize the skills and contributions of individual members?		
12. Do you use emblems such as T-shirts or hats to help people identify with the team and its values?		

If you answered yes to most of these questions, your team in all likelihood has a strong sense of team identity. If you answered no to more than three of these questions, you might want to brainstorm ways to strengthen your group's team identity. If appropriate, consider asking for guidance from your supervisor, team sponsor, or colleagues. You might also consider asking the team for guidance.

RESOLVING A DISAGREEMENT

Use this worksheet to diagnose a disagreement among members and to plan a discussion of how to "get unstuck."

Describe the disagreement.

Diagnose the disagreement. (*Who is involved in the disagreement? What's at stake for this team member?*)

Team member	What's at stake for this team member?
1.	1.
2.	2.
3.	3.

What's at stake here for you?

Plan the right setting for a discussion of the disagreement.

Script a discussion about the disagreement. (*What do you plan to say? How will others respond?*)

What you plan to say	How others may respond
1.	1.
2.	2.
3.	3.

Generate alternative solutions. (*Team members should have an opportunity to offer possible solutions first. Generate a dialogue to explore solutions and examine why each solution is important.*)

Solutions	How/why this solution adds value
1.	1.
2.	2.
3.	3.

Points to keep in mind: (*We are all on the same team. Be inventive in creating solutions that take all critical issues into account.*)

GROUPTHINK ASSESSMENT

Evaluate how well you are using strategies to ensure that your team resists groupthink.

	Questions	Yes	No
1.	Do you and the members of your team know the symptoms of groupthink?		
2.	Have you issued early cautions to your team about the nature and dangers of groupthink?		
3.	Have you established a process for detecting symptoms of groupthink in your team?		
4.	Have you empowered a few people on your team to objectively represent dissenting ideas and data?		
5.	Have you taken steps to ensure that dissent is tolerated and protected, and that dissenters have the freedom to voice contrary views?		
6.	Have you appointed a devil's advocate to challenge all assumptions associated with the group's favored options?		
7.	Do people seem to feel confident expressing dissenting views?		
8.	Do team members feel comfortable hearing others express dissenting views?		

If you answered no to any question, develop a plan for helping your team combat groupthink. Write your ideas in the space below.

Test Yourself

This section offers ten multiple-choice questions to help you identify your baseline knowledge of team management.

Answers to the questions are given at the end of the test.

1. During your weekly team meeting, a heated debate emerges over a particular project your team is working on. You notice that not everyone seems to be participating in the debate. What might you do?

  a. Stop the free flow of conversation and ask if anyone else wants to contribute or is feeling left out.

  b. Stop the conversation and then go around the table to give each person a chance to talk.

  c. After the meeting, poll the team members to see if anyone was hesitant to speak up.

2. Your team members disagree about how best to carry out a particular task. What should you do to handle the disagreement?

  a. Provide a resolution yourself, such as declaring the right way to carry out the task.

  b. Encourage team members to find common ground and explore new possibilities.

c. Let the most persuasive team member determine the out-come of the conflict.

3. You want to encourage active listening during an intense discussion about a conflict within your team. What action might you take?

a. Encourage team members to restate the views of their colleagues and build on those points.

b. Let people know that it's okay to interrupt each other if they need to vent strong emotions.

c. Encourage people to restate the reasons behind their opinions if other team members express confusion or frustration.

4. Your team is evaluating ideas generated during a brainstorming session and ruling out unlikely proposed solutions to a problem. Which kind of thinking is the team engaging in?

a. Divergent thinking.

b. Convergent thinking.

5. Your team is having trouble making a difficult decision. Discussions are going around in circles, and people are rigidly adhering to their positions. Which of the following is the best course of action for you to take?

a. Ask for a vote and then make the decision based on majority rule.

b. Look for smaller areas of agreement on which to build larger decisions.

c. Don't let people get distracted by worrying about the consequences of failing to make a decision.

6. You've assigned Joe, an employee, to lead a team charged with managing a special project. But you've begun noticing signs that Joe is not leading his team effectively. Which of the following is *not* likely a sign of ineffective leadership on Joe's part?

a. Members of Joe's team aren't contributing ideas and opinions during meetings and decision-making sessions.

b. People aren't able to explain why the team's project is important to the company.

c. Joe is giving as many responsibilities as possible to the individuals who are taking part in his team.

7. In the past few team meetings, you've felt that members were neglecting to consider enough alternatives when making decisions and were discounting individuals who expressed minority views. What condition do you suspect your team is beginning to suffer?

a. Decision-making paralysis.

b. Limited team participation.

c. Groupthink.

8. Members of your team don't seem to feel mutually accountable to one another for the team's objectives, and they're not collaborating or sharing information as much as you think they should. Which of the following actions might you take to strengthen team identity?

a. Avoid integrating newcomers, since the presence of strangers can increase awkwardness in a team.

b. Publicly acknowledge the value of differences among team members and explain how those differences serve the team's goal.

c. Avoid implanting any sense of urgency, so team members can focus on forging the bonds necessary for team identity.

9. You're a member of a team led by someone else, and you believe that the team leader isn't delegating enough. What might you do?

a. Point out to the team leader that he or she is acting too much like a traditional boss.

b. Bring in an outside facilitator to advocate the benefits of delegation for the leader.

c. Volunteer to share the team's workload.

10. You've spotted signs of groupthink in your team. Which of the following actions might you take to combat this dangerous tendency?

a. Explain that groupthink can seriously damage a team's ability to come to agreement on important issues.

b. Empower several team members to provide objective evidence supporting the majority's opinions.

c. Appoint a team member to challenge the assumptions and conclusions of the majority.

Answers to test questions

1, b. Some team members may hesitate to interrupt a debate to add their input. When you structure time for everyone to participate, the team benefits by hearing each member's opinion on the issue at hand.

2, b. When team members experience conflict, you should encourage them to find common ground and explore new possibilities. In this case, you might say, "You both want the same result here—a task finished correctly. But you're recommending different ways to get there. Let's discuss the pros and cons of the two different approaches you're arguing over, as well as bring some additional alternatives into the picture. That way, we'll stand a better chance of selecting the best solution."

3, a. Referring back to and building on points made earlier is one effective practice for active listening. Others include controlling behavior that suggests a lack of interest (such as fidgeting), developing questions that encourage a speaker to expand on his or her ideas, and inviting speakers to explain the reasons behind their opinions. Active listening enables people with different perspectives and skills to voice their opinions, which the team needs to make the best decisions.

4, b. During convergent thinking, a team assesses the value of all the ideas generated during divergent thinking to determine which are worth pursuing, given resource constraints and other realities that must be considered. Helping your team move from divergent to convergent thinking is a good way to promote creativity.

5, b. By breaking the decision into smaller pieces that members can agree on, you may make it easier for members to agree on the larger decision. For example, suppose the team is trying to select one of three product designs and can't seem to come to agreement. Focus members' attention on smaller aspects of the decision, for instance, by asking: "What are the most important features that the new product needs to have?" If members can agree on the answer to that question, they may find it easier to agree on the selection of the product design.

6, c. The fact that Joe is giving as many responsibilities as possible to his team members is *not* a sign of ineffective leadership on his part, because a good leader does delegate. If Joe were taking on more tasks and responsibilities than his team members were, you could conclude that he was not leading effectively. Many new team leaders who are used to being individual contributors—doing all the work themselves—have trouble learning to delegate once they begin leading a team.

7, c. Groupthink is a condition that can occur when members of a group think alike to the point where they become unwilling to raise objections or concerns about a project—even though those concerns are legitimate and based on hard data. Groupthink curtails critical thinking and debate, which are two essential ingredients for an effective team.

8, b. By emphasizing how differences within the team serve the team's common goal, you can help strengthen team identity. Additional strategies for enhancing team identity include implanting a sense of urgency, encouraging collaborative work, and quickly integrating newcomers in team projects so they feel welcome and integrated.

9, c. Delegating is essential for any team, because it enables the leader to leverage members' diverse skills, experience, and knowledge. By volunteering to share the workload, you can boost your chances of encouraging the team leader to delegate more.

10, c. By bringing in a devil's advocate, you help ensure that dissenting views are represented in the team and force majority members to deal with facts and ideas that conflict with their own. Providing a devil's advocate is a powerful antidote to groupthink.

To Learn More

Articles

Brett, Jeanne, Kristin Behfar, and Mary C. Kern. "Managing Multi-cultural Teams." *Harvard Business Review*, November 2006.

Multicultural teams offer a number of advantages to international firms, including deep knowledge of different product markets, culturally sensitive customer service, and twenty-four-hour work rotations. But those advantages may be outweighed by problems stemming from cultural differences, which can seriously impair the effectiveness of a team or even bring it to a stalemate. The most successful teams and managers, the authors found, dealt with multicultural challenges in one of four ways: adaptation (acknowledging cultural gaps openly and working around them), structural intervention (changing the shape or makeup of the team), managerial intervention (setting norms early or bringing in a higher-level manager), and exit (removing a team member when other options have failed).

Gary, Loren. "Bury Your Opinion, Shortchange Your Team." *Harvard Management Update*, May 2003.

Management literature tends to focus on the kinds of conflict characterized by interpersonal hostility. But submerged or silenced conflicts and differences of opinion are just as dangerous—and may be even more widespread. And when the leaders who are in place to deal with those conflicts are unaware of their own differences of opinion and are unable to address them, the rest of the unit pays the price. Therefore, the senior executives—the sources of handling conflict in any leadership team—need to know how to deal with their personal conflicts as well as how to deal with their team's conflicts. Also covered: Three books that shed light on this topic, all of which prove that avoiding conflicts may be more harmful in the long run than acknowledging differences up front.

Kling, Jim. "Tension in Teams." *Harvard Management Communication Letter*, July 2000.

Conflict is inevitable in teams, and it is often seen as difficult and uncomfortable. Most people try to avoid conflict altogether, but that can cause problems in the long run. Instead, some experts suggest using team conflict to encourage creative solutions. For this to work, team leaders need to set ground rules such as confronting conflict directly and not allowing it to get personal. A team leader's own behavior is crucial to directing the behavior of the team.

"Managing Teams for High Performance." *Harvard Management Update* (article collection), September 2007.

How do you build teams? What's the best way to manage global teams and diverse teams? How can you take your team to the next level in terms of creativity and effectiveness? The thirteen articles in this *Harvard Management Update* collection provide readers with a comprehensive yet concise resource for developing, managing, and enhancing all types of team endeavors. The five articles in the first section, "Building Team Trust and Cohesiveness," range from increasing your team's emotional intelligence to the pitfalls of too much team camaraderie. The four articles in "Managing Dispersed and Cross-Functional Teams" offer critical insights and practices for taking your team to a global—and even virtual—arena. The authors of the four articles in the final section, "Powering Up Team Creativity and Effectiveness," share best practices gleaned from their research in leadership, psychology, and creativity. Whether you've been a team leader for years or are about to embark on your first team project, you'll find new approaches and practical tips for team success in this article collection.

Michelman, Paul. "Building and Leading Your Team." *Harvard Management Update*, May 2005.

What are the hallmarks of effective senior-team leaders? Not only do they accept that tension and competition are unavoidable, they embrace them, even encourage them. More important, they are able to channel this conflict toward a common good. In the upper reaches of large organizations, teams include executives with billion-dollar responsibilities. These executives have their own strategic priorities, are competing for sometimes scarce resources, and may well be jockeying for positions in the succession queue. To help senior-team leaders manage the tensions and extract top performance, Harvard Business School professor Linda A. Hill has developed a checklist of the key levers for senior-team leaders.

Sethi, Rajesh, Daniel C. Smith, and C. Whan Park. "How to Kill a Team's Creativity." *Harvard Business Review,* August 2002.

Diversity, cohesiveness, and autonomy may seem critical to the creative work that teams do. But new research shows that too much of those factors can thwart innovation.

Books

Hackman, J. Richard. *Leading Teams: Setting the Stage for Great Performances.* Boston: Harvard Business School Press, 2002.

"Leading teams" is not about subscribing to a specific formula or leadership style, says Hackman. Rather, it is about applying a concise set of guiding principles to each unique group situation, and doing so in the leader's own idiosyncratic way. Based on extensive research and using compelling examples ranging from orchestras to airline cockpit crews, *Leading Teams* identifies five essential conditions—a stable team, a clear and engaging direction, an enabling team structure, a supportive organizational context, and the availability of competent coaching—that greatly enhance the likelihood of team success. The book offers a practical framework that leaders can use to muster personal skills and organizational resources to create and sustain the five key conditions, and shows how those conditions can launch a team onto a trajectory of increasing effectiveness.

Harvard Business School Publishing. *Harvard Business Review on Teams That Succeed.* Boston: Harvard Business School Press, 2004.

Managers at all levels strive to develop effective teams while avoiding the pitfalls so common in team management. This invaluable collection of articles explores teamwork from a variety of angles, including emotional intelligence, creativity, and decision making. Every reader will gain insight on how to create and manage teams that work efficiently, effectively, and collaboratively.

Harvard Business School Publishing. *Teams That Click: The Results-Driven Manager Series*. Boston: Harvard Business School Press, 2004.

Managers are under increasing pressure to deliver better results faster than the competition. But meeting today's tough challenges requires complete mastery of a full array of management skills, from communicating and coaching to public speaking and managing people. The Results-Driven Manager series is designed to help time-pressed managers hone and polish the skills they need most. Concise, action oriented, and packed with invaluable strategies and tools, these timely guides help managers improve their job performance today—and give them the edge they need to become the leaders of tomorrow. *Teams That Click* urges managers to identify and select the right mix of people, get team members on board, avoid people-management pitfalls, devise effective reward systems, and boost productivity and performance.

eLearning

Harvard Business School Publishing. *Influencing and Motivating Others.* Boston: Harvard Business School Publishing, 2001.

Have you ever noticed how some people seem to have a natural ability to stir people to action? *Influencing and Motivating Others* provides actionable lessons on getting better results from direct reports (influencing performance), greater cooperation from your peers (lateral leadership), and stronger support from your own boss and senior management (persuasion). Managers will learn the secrets of "lateral leadership" (leading peers), negotiation and persuasion skills, and how to distinguish between effective and ineffective motivation methods. Through interactive cases, expert guidance, and activities for immediate application at work, this program helps managers to assess their ability to effectively persuade others, measure motivation skills, and enhance employee performance.

Harvard Business School Publishing. *Managing Virtual Teams.* Boston: Harvard Business School Publishing, 2000.

This program will prepare you to successfully work with and lead a virtual team. You will understand the four factors that make up an efficient and effective virtual team:

- Great people

- Effective communication

- Appropriate technology

- A shared vision and process

Through interactive role play, expert guidance, and activities for immediate application, this workshop will help you understand and improve your ability to work and communicate through virtual channels. Pre- and post-assessments and additional resources complete the workshop, preparing you to lead a virtual team.

Sources for Managing Teams

The following sources aided in development of this book:

Donnellon, Anne. *Team Talk: The Power of Language in Team Dynamics*. Boston: Harvard Business School Press, 1996.

Harrington-Mackin, Deborah. *Keeping the Team Going*. New York: American Management Association, 1996.

Harvard Business School Publishing. *Creating Teams with an Edge*. Boston: Harvard Business School Press, 2004.

Katzenbach, Jon R., and Douglas K. Smith. *The Wisdom of Teams: Creating the High-Performance Organization*. Boston: Harvard Business School Press, 1993.

Maddux, Robert B. *Team Building: An Exercise in Leadership*. Menlo Park, CA: Crisp Publications, 1992.

Mankin, Don, Susan G. Cohen, and Tora K. Bikson. *Teams and Technology: Fulfilling the Promise of the New Organization*. Boston: Harvard Business School Press, 1996.

Notes

Notes

Notes

Notes

Notes

Notes

Notes

How to Order

Harvard Business School Press publications are available world-wide from your local bookseller or online retailer.

You can also call:
1-800-668-6780

Our product consultants are available to help you 8:00 a.m.–6:00 p.m., Monday–Friday, Eastern Time. Outside the U.S. and Canada, call: 617-783-7450.

Please call about special discounts for quantities greater than ten.

You can order online at:
www.HBSPress.org